Client Record Book: Organize and Manage Your Business

BUSINESS NAME: ....

PHONE NUMBER: ....

EMAIL ID: ....

ADDRESS: ....

....

....

Calendar 2022

January

S	M	T	W	T	F	S
						1
2	3	4	5	6	7	8
9	10	11	12	13	14	15
16	17	18	19	20	21	22
23	24	25	26	27	28	29
30	31					

February

S	M	T	W	T	F	S
		1	2	3	4	5
6	7	8	9	10	11	12
13	14	15	16	17	18	19
20	21	22	23	24	25	26
27	28					

March

S	M	T	W	T	F	S
		1	2	3	4	5
6	7	8	9	10	11	12
13	14	15	16	17	18	19
20	21	22	23	24	25	26
27	28	29	30	31		

Notes

_____

_____

_____

_____

_____

_____

_____

_____

_____

_____

_____

_____

_____

Calendar 2022

April

S	M	T	W	T	F	S
					1	2
3	4	5	6	7	8	9
10	11	12	13	14	15	16
17	18	19	20	21	22	23
24	25	26	27	28	29	30

May

S	M	T	W	T	F	S
1	2	3	4	5	6	7
8	9	10	11	12	13	14
15	16	17	18	19	20	21
22	23	24	25	26	27	28
29	30	31				

June

S	M	T	W	T	F	S
			1	2	3	4
5	6	7	8	9	10	11
12	13	14	15	16	17	18
19	20	21	22	23	24	25
26	27	28	29	30		

Notes

Calendar 2022

July

S	M	T	W	T	F	S
					1	2
3	4	5	6	7	8	9
10	11	12	13	14	15	16
17	18	19	20	21	22	23
24	25	26	27	28	29	30
31						

August

S	M	T	W	T	F	S
	1	2	3	4	5	6
7	8	9	10	11	12	13
14	15	16	17	18	19	20
21	22	23	24	25	26	27
28	29	30	31			

September

S	M	T	W	T	F	S
				1	2	3
4	5	6	7	8	9	10
11	12	13	14	15	16	17
18	19	20	21	22	23	24
25	26	27	28	29	30	

Notes

_____

_____

_____

_____

_____

_____

_____

_____

_____

_____

_____

_____

_____

_____

Calendar 2022

October

S	M	T	W	T	F	S
						1
2	3	4	5	6	7	8
9	10	11	12	13	14	15
16	17	18	19	20	21	22
23	24	25	26	27	28	29
30	31					

November

S	M	T	W	T	F	S
		1	2	3	4	5
6	7	8	9	10	11	12
13	14	15	16	17	18	19
20	21	22	23	24	25	26
27	28	29	30			

December

S	M	T	W	T	F	S
				1	2	3
4	5	6	7	8	9	10
11	12	13	14	15	16	17
18	19	20	21	22	23	24
25	26	27	28	29	30	31

Notes

INDEX

Page	Client Name
1	
2	
3	
4	
5	
6	
7	
8	
9	
10	
11	
12	
13	
14	
15	
16	
17	
18	
19	
20	
21	
22	
23	
24	
25	

INDEX

Page	Client Name
26	
27	
28	
29	
30	
31	
32	
33	
34	
35	
36	
37	
38	
39	
40	
41	
42	
43	
44	
45	
46	
47	
48	
49	
50	

INDEX

Page	Client Name
51	
52	
53	
54	
55	
56	
57	
58	
59	
60	
61	
62	
63	
64	
65	
66	
67	
68	
69	
70	
71	
72	
73	
74	
75	

INDEX

Page	Client Name
76	
77	
78	
79	
80	
81	
82	
83	
84	
85	
86	
87	
88	
89	
90	
91	
92	
93	
94	
95	
96	
97	
98	
99	
100	

Client Record Book

NAME ....

CONTACT NO. ....

EMAIL ID ....

ADDRESS ....

....

NOTES ....

....

....

#	Date	Description of Service	Price	Notes

Client Record Book

NAME   ....

CONTACT NO.   ....

EMAIL ID   ....

ADDRESS   ....

              ....

NOTES   ....

              ....

              ....

#	Date	Description of Service	Price	Notes

Client Record Book

NAME ....

CONTACT NO. ....

EMAIL ID ....

ADDRESS ....

....

NOTES ....

....

....

#	Date	Description of Service	Price	Notes

Client Record Book

NAME ....

CONTACT NO. ....

EMAIL ID ....

ADDRESS ....

....

NOTES ....

....

....

#	Date	Description of Service	Price	Notes

Client Record Book

NAME ....

CONTACT NO. ....

EMAIL ID ....

ADDRESS ....

....

NOTES ....

....

....

#	Date	Description of Service	Price	Notes

Client Record Book

NAME ....

CONTACT NO. ....

EMAIL ID ....

ADDRESS ....

....

NOTES ....

....

....

#	Date	Description of Service	Price	Notes

Client Record Book

NAME ....

CONTACT NO. ....

EMAIL ID ....

ADDRESS ....

....

NOTES ....

....

....

#	Date	Description of Service	Price	Notes

Client Record Book

NAME ....

CONTACT NO. ....

EMAIL ID ....

ADDRESS ....

....

NOTES ....

....

....

#	Date	Description of Service	Price	Notes

Client Record Book

NAME ....

CONTACT NO. ....

EMAIL ID ....

ADDRESS ....

....

NOTES ....

....

....

#	Date	Description of Service	Price	Notes

Client Record Book

NAME ....

CONTACT NO. ....

EMAIL ID ....

ADDRESS ....

....

NOTES ....

....

....

#	Date	Description of Service	Price	Notes

Client Record Book

NAME ....

CONTACT NO. ....

EMAIL ID ....

ADDRESS ....

....

NOTES ....

....

....

#	Date	Description of Service	Price	Notes

Client Record Book

NAME ....

CONTACT NO. ....

EMAIL ID ....

ADDRESS ....

....

NOTES ....

....

....

#	Date	Description of Service	Price	Notes

Client Record Book

NAME ....

CONTACT NO. ....

EMAIL ID ....

ADDRESS ....

....

NOTES ....

....

....

#	Date	Description of Service	Price	Notes

Client Record Book

NAME ....

CONTACT NO. ....

EMAIL ID ....

ADDRESS ....

....

NOTES ....

....

....

#	Date	Description of Service	Price	Notes

Client Record Book

NAME ....

CONTACT NO. ....

EMAIL ID ....

ADDRESS ....

....

NOTES ....

....

....

#	Date	Description of Service	Price	Notes

Client Record Book

NAME ....

CONTACT NO. ....

EMAIL ID ....

ADDRESS ....

....

NOTES ....

....

....

#	Date	Description of Service	Price	Notes

Client Record Book

NAME ....

CONTACT NO. ....

EMAIL ID ....

ADDRESS ....

....

NOTES ....

....

....

#	Date	Description of Service	Price	Notes

Client Record Book

NAME ....

CONTACT NO. ....

EMAIL ID ....

ADDRESS ....

....

NOTES ....

....

....

#	Date	Description of Service	Price	Notes

Client Record Book

NAME ....

CONTACT NO. ....

EMAIL ID ....

ADDRESS ....

....

NOTES ....

....

....

#	Date	Description of Service	Price	Notes

Client Record Book

NAME ....

CONTACT NO. ....

EMAIL ID ....

ADDRESS ....

....

NOTES ....

....

....

#	Date	Description of Service	Price	Notes

Client Record Book

NAME ....

CONTACT NO. ....

EMAIL ID ....

ADDRESS ....

....

NOTES ....

....

....

#	Date	Description of Service	Price	Notes

Client Record Book

NAME ....

CONTACT NO. ....

EMAIL ID ....

ADDRESS ....

....

NOTES ....

....

....

#	Date	Description of Service	Price	Notes

Client Record Book

NAME ....

CONTACT NO. ....

EMAIL ID ....

ADDRESS ....

....

NOTES ....

....

....

#	Date	Description of Service	Price	Notes

Client Record Book

NAME ....

CONTACT NO. ....

EMAIL ID ....

ADDRESS ....

....

NOTES ....

....

....

#	Date	Description of Service	Price	Notes

Client Record Book

NAME ....

CONTACT NO. ....

EMAIL ID ....

ADDRESS ....

....

NOTES ....

....

....

#	Date	Description of Service	Price	Notes

Client Record Book

NAME ....

CONTACT NO. ....

EMAIL ID ....

ADDRESS ....

....

NOTES ....

....

....

#	Date	Description of Service	Price	Notes

Client Record Book

NAME ....

CONTACT NO. ....

EMAIL ID ....

ADDRESS ....

....

NOTES ....

....

....

#	Date	Description of Service	Price	Notes

Client Record Book

NAME ....

CONTACT NO. ....

EMAIL ID ....

ADDRESS ....

....

NOTES ....

....

....

#	Date	Description of Service	Price	Notes

Client Record Book

NAME ....

CONTACT NO. ....

EMAIL ID ....

ADDRESS ....

....

NOTES ....

....

....

#	Date	Description of Service	Price	Notes

Client Record Book

NAME ....

CONTACT NO. ....

EMAIL ID ....

ADDRESS ....

....

NOTES ....

....

....

#	Date	Description of Service	Price	Notes

Client Record Book

NAME ....

CONTACT NO. ....

EMAIL ID ....

ADDRESS ....

....

NOTES ....

....

....

#	Date	Description of Service	Price	Notes

Client Record Book

NAME ....

CONTACT NO. ....

EMAIL ID ....

ADDRESS ....

....

NOTES ....

....

....

#	Date	Description of Service	Price	Notes

Client Record Book

NAME ....

CONTACT NO. ....

EMAIL ID ....

ADDRESS ....

....

NOTES ....

....

....

#	Date	Description of Service	Price	Notes

Client Record Book

NAME ....

CONTACT NO. ....

EMAIL ID ....

ADDRESS ....

....

NOTES ....

....

....

#	Date	Description of Service	Price	Notes

Client Record Book

NAME ....

CONTACT NO. ....

EMAIL ID ....

ADDRESS ....

....

NOTES ....

....

....

#	Date	Description of Service	Price	Notes

Client Record Book

NAME ....

CONTACT NO. ....

EMAIL ID ....

ADDRESS ....

....

NOTES ....

....

....

#	Date	Description of Service	Price	Notes

Client Record Book

NAME ....

CONTACT NO. ....

EMAIL ID ....

ADDRESS ....

....

NOTES ....

....

....

#	Date	Description of Service	Price	Notes

Client Record Book

NAME ....

CONTACT NO. ....

EMAIL ID ....

ADDRESS ....

....

NOTES ....

....

....

#	Date	Description of Service	Price	Notes

Client Record Book

NAME ....

CONTACT NO. ....

EMAIL ID ....

ADDRESS ....

....

NOTES ....

....

....

#	Date	Description of Service	Price	Notes

Client Record Book

NAME ....

CONTACT NO. ....

EMAIL ID ....

ADDRESS ....

....

NOTES ....

....

....

#	Date	Description of Service	Price	Notes

Client Record Book

NAME ....

CONTACT NO. ....

EMAIL ID ....

ADDRESS ....

....

NOTES ....

....

....

#	Date	Description of Service	Price	Notes

Client Record Book

NAME ....

CONTACT NO. ....

EMAIL ID ....

ADDRESS ....

....

NOTES ....

....

....

#	Date	Description of Service	Price	Notes

Client Record Book

NAME ....

CONTACT NO. ....

EMAIL ID ....

ADDRESS ....

....

NOTES ....

....

....

#	Date	Description of Service	Price	Notes

Client Record Book

NAME   ....

CONTACT NO.   ....

EMAIL ID   ....

ADDRESS   ....

                     ....

NOTES   ....

                     ....

                     ....

#	Date	Description of Service	Price	Notes

Client Record Book

NAME ....

CONTACT NO. ....

EMAIL ID ....

ADDRESS ....

....

NOTES ....

....

....

#	Date	Description of Service	Price	Notes

Client Record Book

NAME ....

CONTACT NO. ....

EMAIL ID ....

ADDRESS ....

....

NOTES ....

....

....

#	Date	Description of Service	Price	Notes

Client Record Book

NAME ....

CONTACT NO. ....

EMAIL ID ....

ADDRESS ....

....

NOTES ....

....

....

#	Date	Description of Service	Price	Notes

Client Record Book

NAME ....

CONTACT NO. ....

EMAIL ID ....

ADDRESS ....

....

NOTES ....

....

....

#	Date	Description of Service	Price	Notes

Client Record Book

NAME ....

CONTACT NO. ....

EMAIL ID ....

ADDRESS ....

....

NOTES ....

....

....

#	Date	Description of Service	Price	Notes

Client Record Book

NAME ....

CONTACT NO. ....

EMAIL ID ....

ADDRESS ....

....

NOTES ....

....

....

#	Date	Description of Service	Price	Notes

Client Record Book

NAME ....

CONTACT NO. ....

EMAIL ID ....

ADDRESS ....

....

NOTES ....

....

....

#	Date	Description of Service	Price	Notes

Client Record Book

NAME ....

CONTACT NO. ....

EMAIL ID ....

ADDRESS ....

....

NOTES ....

....

....

#	Date	Description of Service	Price	Notes

Client Record Book

NAME ....

CONTACT NO. ....

EMAIL ID ....

ADDRESS ....

....

NOTES ....

....

....

#	Date	Description of Service	Price	Notes

Client Record Book

NAME ....

CONTACT NO. ....

EMAIL ID ....

ADDRESS ....

....

NOTES ....

....

....

#	Date	Description of Service	Price	Notes

Client Record Book

NAME ....

CONTACT NO. ....

EMAIL ID ....

ADDRESS ....

....

NOTES ....

....

....

#	Date	Description of Service	Price	Notes

Client Record Book

NAME ....

CONTACT NO. ....

EMAIL ID ....

ADDRESS ....

....

NOTES ....

....

....

#	Date	Description of Service	Price	Notes

Client Record Book

NAME ....

CONTACT NO. ....

EMAIL ID ....

ADDRESS ....

....

NOTES ....

....

....

#	Date	Description of Service	Price	Notes

Client Record Book

NAME   ....

CONTACT NO.   ....

EMAIL ID   ....

ADDRESS   ....

                        ....

NOTES   ....

                        ....

                        ....

#	Date	Description of Service	Price	Notes

Client Record Book

NAME ....

CONTACT NO. ....

EMAIL ID ....

ADDRESS ....

....

NOTES ....

....

....

#	Date	Description of Service	Price	Notes

Client Record Book

NAME   ....

CONTACT NO.   ....

EMAIL ID   ....

ADDRESS   ....

              ....

NOTES   ....

              ....

              ....

#	Date	Description of Service	Price	Notes

Client Record Book

NAME ....

CONTACT NO. ....

EMAIL ID ....

ADDRESS ....

....

NOTES ....

....

....

#	Date	Description of Service	Price	Notes

Client Record Book

NAME ....

CONTACT NO. ....

EMAIL ID ....

ADDRESS ....

....

NOTES ....

....

....

#	Date	Description of Service	Price	Notes

Client Record Book

NAME ....

CONTACT NO. ....

EMAIL ID ....

ADDRESS ....

....

NOTES ....

....

....

#	Date	Description of Service	Price	Notes

Client Record Book

NAME   ....

CONTACT NO.   ....

EMAIL ID   ....

ADDRESS   ....

               ....

NOTES   ....

               ....

               ....

#	Date	Description of Service	Price	Notes

Client Record Book

NAME ....

CONTACT NO. ....

EMAIL ID ....

ADDRESS ....

....

NOTES ....

....

....

#	Date	Description of Service	Price	Notes

Client Record Book

NAME ....

CONTACT NO. ....

EMAIL ID ....

ADDRESS ....

....

NOTES ....

....

....

#	Date	Description of Service	Price	Notes

Client Record Book

NAME ....

CONTACT NO. ....

EMAIL ID ....

ADDRESS ....

....

NOTES ....

....

....

#	Date	Description of Service	Price	Notes

Client Record Book

NAME ....

CONTACT NO. ....

EMAIL ID ....

ADDRESS ....

....

NOTES ....

....

....

#	Date	Description of Service	Price	Notes

Client Record Book

NAME ....

CONTACT NO. ....

EMAIL ID ....

ADDRESS ....

....

NOTES ....

....

....

#	Date	Description of Service	Price	Notes

Client Record Book

NAME ....

CONTACT NO. ....

EMAIL ID ....

ADDRESS ....

....

NOTES ....

....

....

#	Date	Description of Service	Price	Notes

Client Record Book

NAME ....

CONTACT NO. ....

EMAIL ID ....

ADDRESS ....

....

NOTES ....

....

....

#	Date	Description of Service	Price	Notes

Client Record Book

NAME ....

CONTACT NO. ....

EMAIL ID ....

ADDRESS ....

....

NOTES ....

....

....

#	Date	Description of Service	Price	Notes

Client Record Book

NAME ....

CONTACT NO. ....

EMAIL ID ....

ADDRESS ....

....

NOTES ....

....

....

#	Date	Description of Service	Price	Notes

Client Record Book

NAME ....

CONTACT NO. ....

EMAIL ID ....

ADDRESS ....

....

NOTES ....

....

....

#	Date	Description of Service	Price	Notes

Client Record Book

NAME ....

CONTACT NO. ....

EMAIL ID ....

ADDRESS ....

....

NOTES ....

....

....

#	Date	Description of Service	Price	Notes

Client Record Book

NAME ....

CONTACT NO. ....

EMAIL ID ....

ADDRESS ....

....

NOTES ....

....

....

#	Date	Description of Service	Price	Notes

Client Record Book

NAME ....

CONTACT NO. ....

EMAIL ID ....

ADDRESS ....

....

NOTES ....

....

....

#	Date	Description of Service	Price	Notes

Client Record Book

NAME ....

CONTACT NO. ....

EMAIL ID ....

ADDRESS ....

....

NOTES ....

....

....

#	Date	Description of Service	Price	Notes

Client Record Book

NAME ....

CONTACT NO. ....

EMAIL ID ....

ADDRESS ....

....

NOTES ....

....

....

#	Date	Description of Service	Price	Notes

Client Record Book

NAME ....

CONTACT NO. ....

EMAIL ID ....

ADDRESS ....

....

NOTES ....

....

....

#	Date	Description of Service	Price	Notes

Client Record Book

NAME ....

CONTACT NO. ....

EMAIL ID ....

ADDRESS ....

....

NOTES ....

....

....

#	Date	Description of Service	Price	Notes

Client Record Book

NAME ....

CONTACT NO. ....

EMAIL ID ....

ADDRESS ....

....

NOTES ....

....

....

#	Date	Description of Service	Price	Notes

Client Record Book

NAME ....

CONTACT NO. ....

EMAIL ID ....

ADDRESS ....

....

NOTES ....

....

....

#	Date	Description of Service	Price	Notes

Client Record Book

NAME ....

CONTACT NO. ....

EMAIL ID ....

ADDRESS ....

....

NOTES ....

....

....

#	Date	Description of Service	Price	Notes

Client Record Book

NAME ....

CONTACT NO. ....

EMAIL ID ....

ADDRESS ....

....

NOTES ....

....

....

#	Date	Description of Service	Price	Notes

Client Record Book

NAME ....

CONTACT NO. ....

EMAIL ID ....

ADDRESS ....

....

NOTES ....

....

....

#	Date	Description of Service	Price	Notes

Client Record Book

NAME ....

CONTACT NO. ....

EMAIL ID ....

ADDRESS ....

....

NOTES ....

....

....

#	Date	Description of Service	Price	Notes

Client Record Book

NAME ....

CONTACT NO. ....

EMAIL ID ....

ADDRESS ....

....

NOTES ....

....

....

#	Date	Description of Service	Price	Notes

Client Record Book

NAME ....

CONTACT NO. ....

EMAIL ID ....

ADDRESS ....

....

NOTES ....

....

....

#	Date	Description of Service	Price	Notes

Client Record Book

NAME ....

CONTACT NO. ....

EMAIL ID ....

ADDRESS ....

....

NOTES ....

....

....

#	Date	Description of Service	Price	Notes

Client Record Book

NAME ....

CONTACT NO. ....

EMAIL ID ....

ADDRESS ....

....

NOTES ....

....

....

#	Date	Description of Service	Price	Notes

Client Record Book

NAME ....

CONTACT NO. ....

EMAIL ID ....

ADDRESS ....

....

NOTES ....

....

....

#	Date	Description of Service	Price	Notes

Client Record Book

NAME ....

CONTACT NO. ....

EMAIL ID ....

ADDRESS ....

....

NOTES ....

....

....

#	Date	Description of Service	Price	Notes

Client Record Book

NAME ....

CONTACT NO. ....

EMAIL ID ....

ADDRESS ....

....

NOTES ....

....

....

#	Date	Description of Service	Price	Notes

Client Record Book

NAME ....

CONTACT NO. ....

EMAIL ID ....

ADDRESS ....

....

NOTES ....

....

....

#	Date	Description of Service	Price	Notes

Client Record Book

NAME ....

CONTACT NO. ....

EMAIL ID ....

ADDRESS ....

....

NOTES ....

....

....

#	Date	Description of Service	Price	Notes

Client Record Book

NAME ....

CONTACT NO. ....

EMAIL ID ....

ADDRESS ....

....

NOTES ....

....

....

#	Date	Description of Service	Price	Notes

Client Record Book

NAME   ....

CONTACT NO.   ....

EMAIL ID   ....

ADDRESS   ....

....

NOTES   ....

....

....

#	Date	Description of Service	Price	Notes

Client Record Book

NAME ....

CONTACT NO. ....

EMAIL ID ....

ADDRESS ....

....

NOTES ....

....

....

#	Date	Description of Service	Price	Notes

Client Record Book

NAME ....

CONTACT NO. ....

EMAIL ID ....

ADDRESS ....

....

NOTES ....

....

....

#	Date	Description of Service	Price	Notes

Made in the USA
Coppell, TX
04 November 2022